GUITAR • VOCAL

STRUM & SING

TOP
CHRISTIAN HITS

Photo courtesy Library of Congress, Prints & Photographs Division
Photograph by Carol M. Highsmith

ISBN 978-1-4950-5875-2

HAL•LEONARD®
CORPORATION
7777 W. BLUEMOUND RD. P.O. BOX 13819 MILWAUKEE, WI 53213

Visit Hal Leonard Online at
www.halleonard.com

CONTENTS

Build Your Kingdom Here

Words and Music by
Rend Collective

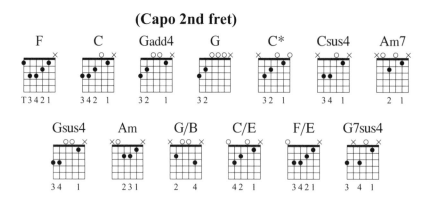

(Capo 2nd fret)

Verse 1

|F |C |F |C
Come set Your rule and reign in our hearts a - gain.

|F |C
In - crease in us, we pray.

|Gadd4 |
Un - veil why we're made.

|F   G |C
Come set our hearts a - blaze with hope,

|F   G |C |
Like wildfire in our very souls.

|F   G |C |Gadd4 | |
Holy Spir - it, come invade us now.

Pre-Chorus 1

|F   C |Gadd4 |
We are Your Church.

|F   C |Gadd4 |C* |Csus4
We need Your pow'r in us.

Verse 2

```
|F            G  |C     |F          G |C
We seek Your king - dom first, we hunger and we thirst,
 |F        G  |C      |G              |
Re - fuse to waste our lives for You're our joy and prize.
  |F        G  |C
To see the cap - tive   hearts released,
   |F        G |C              |
The hurt, the sick, the poor at peace,
|F         G |C              |G         |        |
 We lay down our lives for heaven's cause.
```

Pre-Chorus 2

```
|F   C      |Gadd4     |
 We  are Your Church.
|F   C      |Gadd4 |C*     |Csus4     |C*      |Csus4
 We  pray: Re - vive this earth.
```

Chorus 1

```
        |G      |Am7       |F      |C
Build Your kingdom here, let the darkness fear.
        |G   |Am7          |F       |G
Show Your mighty hand, heal our streets and land.
C       |G      |Am7         |F   |C
Set Your Church on fire, win this nation back.
        |G      |Am7             |F        |G
Change the atmos - phere, build Your kingdom here,
  |C*       Csus4 |C*      Csus4 |C*       Csus4 |C*
We pray.
```

Verse 3

```
   |F              |C          |F            |C
Un - leash Your kingdom's pow'r, reach - ing the near and far.
   |F       |C       |G             |
No force of hell can stop Your beauty changing hearts.
   |F            |C
You made us for much more than this.
   |F            |C         |
A - wake the kingdom seed in us.
|F         |C           |G       |      |
 Fill us with the strength and love of Christ.
```

Pre-Chorus 3

```
|F   C        |Gadd4    |
We are Your Church.
|F    C       |Gadd4 |C*         Csus4 |C
We   are the hope on earth.
```

Chorus 2

```
            |G    |Am7       |F      |C
Build Your kingdom here, let the darkness fear.
            |G    |Am7          |F      |G
Show Your mighty hand, heal our streets and land.
C     |G      |Am7        |F    |C
Set Your Church on fire, win this nation back.
            |G    |Am7             |F    |G      |
Change the atmos - phere, build Your kingdom here, we
```

Bridge

```
|C       Gsus4 |C      Gsus4 |Am      Gsus4 |Am       Gsus4    |
pray.
 Oh, _____      oh, _____      oh, ____
|C       Gsus4 |C      Gsus4 |Am      Gsus4 |Am        G/B      |
_____       oh, _____      oh, ____
|C        G/B |C       C/E |F       F/E |F           G        |
_____       oh, _____      oh, ____
|Am       G |Am      G/B |C        |          |          |
_____       oh, _____      oh. _____
```

Outro-Chorus

```
            |G    |Am7       |F      |C
Build Your kingdom here, let the darkness fear.
            |G    |Am7          |F      |G
Show Your mighty hand, heal our streets and land.
C     |G      |Am7        |F    |C
Set Your Church on fire, win this nation back.
            |G    |Am7             |F    |G
Change the atmos - phere, build Your kingdom here,
  |C    G7sus4 |C      G7sus4 |C        G7sus4 |C         ||
We pray.
```

6

Greater

Words and Music by Bart Millard,
Mike Scheuchzer, Nathan Cochran,
Robby Shaffer, Barry Graul,
David Garcia and Ben Glover

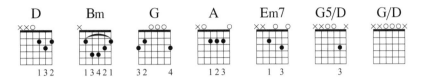

Intro

|N.C. | | | |
Ooh, _____   ooh, _____
|D | | |
Ooh, _____   ooh. _____

Verse 1

           |D |
Bring your tired and bring your shame,

          | |
Bring your guilt and bring your pain.

       | |
Don't you know that's not your name?
|Bm   G |D
You will always be much more to Me.

Pre-Chorus 1

         |A
And ev'ry day I wrestle with

    |Bm
The voices that keep telling me

  |G |
I'm not right, but that's alright.

Chorus 1

|D   Em7 |Bm

'Cause I hear a voice, and He calls me redeemed

| G |D

When others say I'll never be enough.

| Em7 |Bm

And greater is the One living inside of me

| G |D

Than he who is living in the world,

|Bm G |D |Bm G |D

In the world, _____ in the world. _____

|Bm   G |D

And greater is the One liv - ing inside of me

|Bm   G |D |

Than he who is living in the world.

Verse 2

|D |

Bring your doubts and bring your fears,

| |

Bring your hurt and bring your tears.

| | |

There'll be no condemnation here.

|Bm   G |D

You are holy, righteous and redeemed.

Pre-Chorus 2

|A

And ev'ry time I fall,

|Bm |G

There'll be those who will call me a mistake.

|

Well, that's okay.

Chorus 2

Repeat Chorus 1

Interlude

```
|D        |              |
```
Oh, _____ oh, _____ *woo!*
```
|        |              G5/D    |
```
Oh, _____ He's greater, He's greater.
```
|D        |              |         |   G/D    |
```
Oh, _____ oh, _____ *woo!* Oh. _____

Bridge

```
‖: D                        |                        |
```
There'll be days I lose the battle; grace says that it doesn't matter
```
|                    |                    |
```
'Cause the cross already won the war. (He's greater, He's greater.)
```
|                    |                    |
```
I am learning to run freely, understanding just how He sees me,
```
|                    |
```
And it makes me love Him more and more.
```
|              N.C.              :‖
```
(He's greater,   He's greater.) Oh! _____

Chorus 3   *Repeat Chorus 1*

Outro

```
|D                   G   |D                        |
```
There'll be days I lose the battle; grace says that it doesn't matter
```
|Bm              G        |D                        |
```
'Cause the cross already won the war. (He's greater, He's greater.)
```
|Bm              G   |D                        |
```
I am learning to run freely, understanding just how He sees me,
```
|Bm                  G            |D
```
And it makes me love Him more and more. Our God is greater
```
   |Bm          G        |D   G/D  D    ‖
```
Than he who is living in the world.

Good Good Father

Words and Music by
Pat Barrett and Anthony Brown

(Capo 2nd fret)

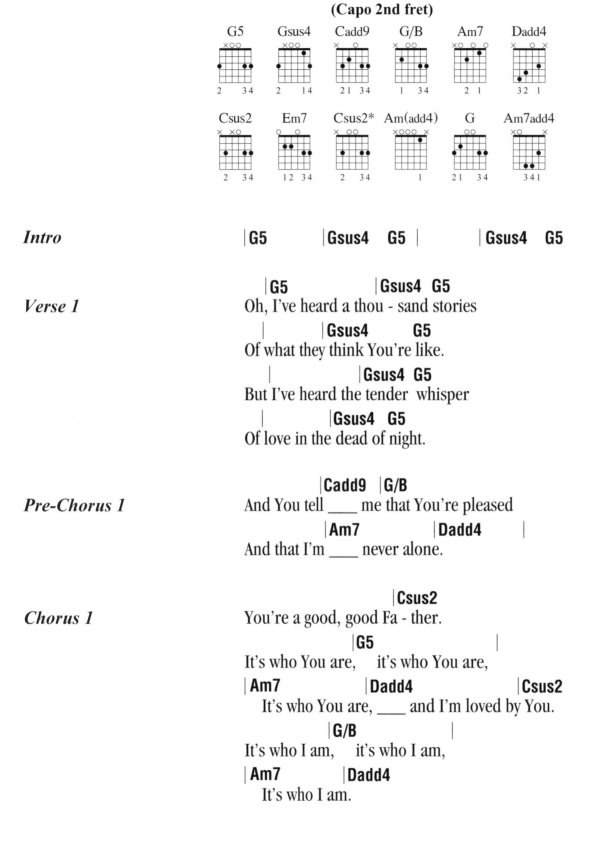

Intro

|G5 |Gsus4   G5 | |Gsus4   G5

Verse 1

|G5 |Gsus4 G5
Oh, I've heard a thou - sand stories

| |Gsus4   G5
Of what they think You're like.

| |Gsus4   G5
But I've heard the tender whisper

| |Gsus4   G5
Of love in the dead of night.

Pre-Chorus 1

|Cadd9 |G/B
And You tell ____ me that You're pleased

|Am7 |Dadd4 |
And that I'm ____ never alone.

Chorus 1

|Csus2
You're a good, good Fa - ther.

|G5 |
It's who You are,   it's who You are,

|Am7 |Dadd4 |Csus2
It's who You are, ____ and I'm loved by You.

|G/B |
It's who I am,   it's who I am,

|Am7 |Dadd4
It's who I am.

Verse 2

         |**G5** |
Oh, and I've ___ seen many searching

     | |
For answers far and wide.

     | |
But I know we're all searching

     | |
For answers only You provide.

Pre-Chorus 2

        |**Cadd9** |**G/B**
'Cause You know ___ just what we need
     |**Am7** |**Dadd4**
Before we say a word.

Chorus 2   *Repeat Chorus 1*

Bridge

        |**Csus2** |**Em7**
Because You are perfect in all of Your ways.
     |**Am7** |**G5**
You are perfect in all of Your ways.
     |**Csus2** |**Em7** |**Dadd4** |
You are perfect in all of Your ways ___ to us.
     |**Csus2** |**Em7**
You are perfect in all of Your ways.
     |**Am7** |**G5**
You are perfect in all of Your ways.
     |**Csus2** |**Em7** |**Dadd4** |
You are perfect in all of Your ways ___ to us.

Verse 3

       |**G5** |**Gsus4** **G5** |
Oh, it's love so unde - niable,
     | |**Gsus4** **G5** |
I, I can hardly speak.
     | |**Gsus4** **G5** |
Peace so unex - plainable,
     | |
I, I can hardly think

Pre-Chorus 3

        |Cadd9 Csus2* |G/B
As You call ___ me   deeper still,

        |Am7 Am(add4) |G/B   G
As You call ___ me   deeper still,

        |Cadd9 Csus2* |G/B   **|Am7**   **|Dadd4**
As You call ___ me   deeper still into love, ___ love, love.

Chorus 3

         |Csus2
You're a good, good Fa - ther.

        |G5   **|**
It's who You are,   it's who You are,

| Am7   **|Dadd4**   **|Csus2**
  It's who You are, ___ and I'm loved by You.

        |G5   **|**
It's who I am,   it's who I am,

| Am7   **|Dadd4**
  It's who I am.

Chorus 4   *Repeat Chorus 3*

Chorus 5

         |Csus2
You're a good, good Fa - ther.

        |G/B   **|**
It's who You are,   it's who You are,

| Am7add4   **|Dadd4**   **|Csus2**
  It's who You are, ___ and I'm loved by You.

        |G/B   **|**
It's who I am,   it's who I am,

| Am7add4   **|Dadd4**
  It's who I am.

Chorus 6

         |Csus2
You're a good, good Fa - ther.

        |G5   **|**
It's who You are,   it's who You are,

|Am7add4   **|Dadd4**   **|Csus2**
  It's who You are, ___ and I'm loved by You.

        |G5   **|**
It's who I am,   it's who I am,

|Am7add4   **|Dadd4**   **|**
  It's who I am.

Outro   **|Csus2**   **|G5**   **|Am7add4** **|Dadd4**   **|Cadd9**   **||**

I Need a Miracle

Words and Music by Mac Powell,
Tai Anderson, David Carr and Mark Lee

(Capo 2nd fret)

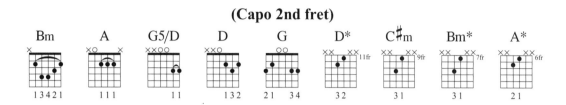

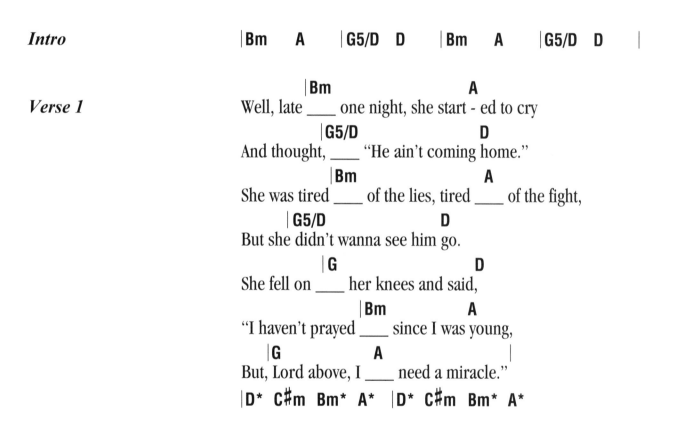

Intro

|Bm   A |G5/D D |Bm   A |G5/D D |

Verse 1

       |Bm   A
Well, late ___ one night, she start - ed to cry
         |G5/D   D
And thought, ___ "He ain't coming home."
        |Bm   A
She was tired ___ of the lies, tired ___ of the fight,
      |G5/D   D
But she didn't wanna see him go.
        |G   D
She fell on ___ her knees and said,
          |Bm   A
"I haven't prayed ___ since I was young,
 |G   A
But, Lord above, I ___ need a miracle."
|D* C#m Bm* A* |D* C#m Bm* A*

Chorus 1

```
        | G            D
Well, no matter who you are
             | A            Bm
And no mat - ter what you've done,
                   | G       D                    | A
There will come ____ a time when you can't make it on ____ your own.
                   | G         D
And in your hour ____ of desper - ation,
                 | A        Bm
Know you're not ____ the only one
            | G          A              | G   D   |
Praying, "Lord, ____ above, I ____ need a miracle.
| Bm   A                    | G   D  | Bm   A
        I need a miracle.
```

Verse 2

```
         | Bm        A              | G5/D     D
He lost ____ his job and all he had in the fall of '0 - 9.
              | Bm          A
Now he feared ____ the worst, that he would lose
         | G5/D           D
His chil - dren and his wife.
            | G            D
So he drove ____ down deep in - to the woods
           | Bm          A
And thought ____ he'd end it all,
         | G           A            | D
And prayed, "Lord above, I ____ need a miracle."
```

Chorus 2   *Repeat Chorus 1*

Bridge 1

```
            |: G          D
La, da, da, ____ da, da, da, da.
            | Bm          A
La, da, da, ____ da, da, da, da.
            | G          D      | A          :|
La, da, da, ____ da, da, da, da. Whoa.
```

Interlude |Bm   A |G5/D   D

                                    |Bm   A
Verse 3   He turned on ___ the radi - o
                                    |G5/D   D
                     To hear a song ___ for the last time.
                                |Bm   A
                     He didn't know what he was looking for,
                                |G5/D   D
                     Or e - ven what he'd find.
                                        |G   D
                     And the song ___ he heard, it gave him hope
                                        |A   Bm |
                     And strength ___ to carry on.
                                    |G   A |G   D |
                     And on ___ that night, they ___ found a miracle.
                     |Bm   A |G   D |Bm   A
                              They found a miracle.

                                        |G   D
Bridge 2   La, da, da, ___ da, da, da, da.
                                    |Bm   A
                     La, da, da, ___ da, da, da, da.
                                        |G   D |A |
                     La, da, da, ___ da, da, da, da. Whoa.

                                            |G   D
Outro   And in your hour ___ of desper - ation,
                                        |A   Bm
                     Know you're not ___ the only one
                                            |G   A |D
                     Praying, "Lord ___ above, I ___ need a miracle.
                              |G   A |D   ‖
                     Lord ___ above, I ___ need a miracle."

Holy Spirit

Words and Music by
Katie Torwalt and Bryan Torwalt

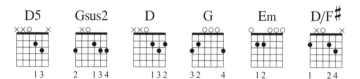

Intro |D5 | |Gsus2 | |

Verse 1
|D5 | |
There's nothing worth more   that could ever come close.
|Gsus2 | |D5 |
No thing can compare,   You're our living hope.
| |Gsus2 | |
Your presence, Lord.

Verse 2
|D5 | |
I've tasted and seen   of the sweetest of loves,
|Gsus2 | |D5 |
Where my heart becomes free   and my shame is un - done.
| |Gsus2 | |
Your presence, Lord.

Chorus 1
|D |
Holy Spirit, You are welcome here.
|G |Em
Come flood this place and fill the atmosphere.
|D |
Your glory, God, is what our hearts long for,
|G |Em |D |
To be overcome by Your presence, Lord.
| |G |Em |
Your presence, Lord.

Verse 3   *Repeat Verse 1*

Verse 4   *Repeat Verse 2*

Bridge

‖: G   D/F♯ |Em   D/F♯ |
Let us become ___ more aware ___ of Your presence.

|G   D/F♯ |Em   D/F♯   :‖ *Play 3 times*
Let us expe - rience the glo - ry of Your goodness.

|G   D/F♯ |Em   D/F♯ |
Let us become ___ more aware ___ of Your presence.

|G   D/F♯ |Em   D/F♯ |Gsus2 | |
Let us expe - rience the glo - ry of Your goodness.

Outro-Chorus

|D |
 Holy Spirit, You are welcome here.

  |G |Em
Come flood this place and fill the atmosphere.

   |D |
Your glory, God, is what our hearts long for,

  |G |Em |D   ‖
To be overcome by Your presence, Lord.

I Am

Words and Music by
David Crowder and Ed Cash

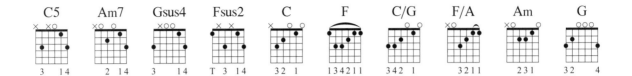

Intro |C5 | |

Verse 1
|C5 | |
There's no space that His love can't reach.
|Am7 | |
There's no place where we can't find peace.
|Gsus4 |Fsus2 | |
There's no end to a - mazing grace.

Verse 2
|C5 | |
Take me in with Your arms spread wide.
|Am7 | |
Take me in like an orphaned child.
|Gsus4 |Fsus2 |
Never let go, never leave my side.

Chorus 1
             |C |Am7 |
I am ___ holding on to You. I am ___ holding on to You.
                 |F | |C5 | |
In the middle of the storm, I am holding on, I am.

Verse 3
|C5 |
Love like this, oh, my God, to find.
    |Am7 | |
I am overwhelmed, what a joy divine.
|Gsus4 | |
Love like this sets our hearts on fire.

Chorus 2

```
         |C            |              |Am7         |
```
I am ___ holding on to You. I am ___ holding on to You.
```
          |F            |                       |C        |
```
In the middle of the storm, I am holding on, I am.   (Oh,   oh.)
```
          |             |              |Am7         |
```
I am ___ holding on to You. I am ___ holding on to You.
```
          |F            |                       |C        |         |
```
In the middle of the storm, I am holding on, I am.   (Oh,   oh.)

Interlude

```
|C5         |              |Fsus2     |            |
```

Bridge

```
      |C           |F             |
```
 This is my resur - rection song.
```
      |C/G          |F/A          |
```
 This is my "Halle - lujah, come!"
```
      |Am           |G            |
```
 This is why it's to You I run.
```
      |C                   |Fsus2         |
```
 There's no space that His love can't reach.
```
      |C/G                    |F/A              |
```
 There's no place where we can't find peace.
```
      |Am              |G          |Fsus2     |
```
 There's no end to a - mazing grace.

Chorus 3

```
         |C            |              |Am7         |
```
I am ___ holding on to You. I am ___ holding on to You.
```
          |F            |
```
In the middle of the storm, I am holding on.
```
          |C            |              |Am7         |
```
I am ___ holding on to You. I am ___ holding on to You.
```
          |F            |
```
In the middle of the storm, I am holding on.

Outro-Chorus

```
         |C            |              |Am7         |
```
I am ___ holding on to You. I am ___ holding on to You.
```
          |F            |
```
In the middle of the storm, I am holding on,
```
         |C            |              |Am7         |
```
I am. ___ (Oh,   oh.) I am. ___ (Oh,   oh.)
```
          |F            |                       |C        ||
```
In the middle of the storm, I am holding on, I am.

Lord, I Need You

Words and Music by Jesse Reeves,
Kristian Stanfill, Matt Maher,
Christy Nockels and Daniel Carson

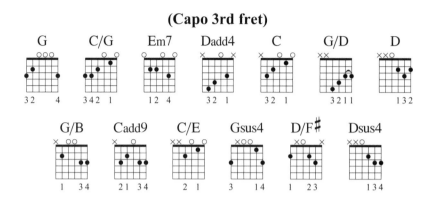

Intro

    |G   C/G |G

Verse 1

C/G |G   C/G |G
Lord, I come, I con - fess,

    |Em7 Dadd4 |C
Bowing here I find my rest.

    |G   C/G |G
Without You I fall a - part.

    |G/D Dadd4 |C |
You're the One   that guides my heart.

Chorus 1

    |G   C/G |G D |
Lord, I need You, oh, I need You.

|Em7 C |G D
 Ev'ry   hour I need You.

    |G/B   Cadd9 |G/D   C/E
My one de - fense, my righteous - ness,

    |G/D   D G |C/G
Oh, God, how I need You.

Verse 2

```
              |G          C/G  |G
Where sin runs deep, Your grace is more.
                   |Em7    D      |C
Where grace is found is where You are.
                 |G        C/G |G
Where You are, Lord, I am   free.
         |G/D   D            |G        |Gsus4
Holi - ness       is Christ in me.
```

Chorus 2

```
              |G          C  |G    D      |
Lord, I need You, oh, I need You.
|Em7  C    |G    D
 Ev'ry   hour I need You.
        |G/B    Cadd9  |G/D          C/E
My one de - fense, my righteous - ness,
         |G/D          D  |G
Oh, God, how I need You.
```

Bridge

```
        |C        G/B    D/F♯ |Em7         |
So teach my song to rise to You
|C            D        |C          |
 When temptation comes my way.
        |         G/B      D/F♯ |Em7        |
When I cannot stand I'll fall on You.
|C            D        |G          |C/G
Jesus, You're my hope and stay.
```

Chorus 3

Repeat Chorus 2

Outro

```
             |G/B    Cadd9  |G/D          C/E
You're my one de - fense, my righteous - ness,
        |G/D          D  |G
Oh, God, how I need You.
        |G/B    Cadd9  |G/D          C/E
My one de - fense, my righteous - ness,
         |G/D       Dsus4  D  |G              ‖
Oh, God, how I need          You.
```

One Thing Remains
(Your Love Never Fails)

Words and Music by Jeremy Riddle,
Brian Johnson and Christa Black

Tune down 1/2 step:
(low to high) E♭-A♭-D♭-G♭-B♭-E♭

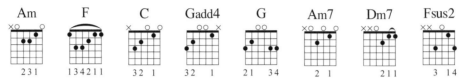

Am   F   C   Gadd4   G   Am7   Dm7   Fsus2

Intro

|Am   F |C   Gadd4 |Am   F |C   Gadd4 |

Verse 1

|F   C |Gadd4 |
Higher than the mountains that I ___ face,
|F   C |Gadd4 |
Stronger than the power of the ___ grave,
|F   C |Gadd4
Constant in the trial and the ___ change,
          |F   C |G
This one thing   remains,
          |F   C |G
This one thing   remains:

Chorus 1

          |Am7   F
Your love ___ never fails, it never gives up,
     |C   G
It never runs out on me.
          |Am7   F
Your love ___ never fails, it never gives up,
     |C   G
It never runs out on me.
          |Am7   F
Your love ___ never fails, it never gives up,
     |C   G
It never runs out on me,
          |Am7   F |C   Gadd4 |
Your love.

Pre-Chorus 1

```
        |F            C          |Gadd4
And on and on and on and on it ___ goes.
          |F              C        |Gadd4
Yes, it overwhelms and satisfies my ___ soul.
           |F          C          |Gadd4
And I'll never ever have to be a - fraid,
                    |F      C          |G
'Cause this one thing     remains:
```

Chorus 2

Repeat Chorus 1

Bridge

```
      |F         C     |G          Dm7
In death, in life, I'm confident and covered by
        |F          C        |G
The pow'r of Your great love.
      |F      C           |G           Dm7
My debt is paid, there's nothing that can separate
        |F          C        |G
My heart from Your great love.
```

Chorus 3

```
            | Am7             F
Your love ___ never fails, it never gives up,
   |C               G
It never runs out on me.
           | Am7             F
Your love ___ never fails, it never gives up,
   |C               G
It never runs out on me.
```

Pre-Chorus 2

Repeat Pre-Chorus 1

Chorus 4

|Am7   F

Your love ___ never fails, it never gives up,

 |C   G

It never runs out on me.

    |Am7   F

Your love ___ never fails, it never gives up,

 |C   G

It never runs out on me.

    |Am7   F

Your love ___ never fails, it never gives up,

 |C   G

It never runs out on me,

  |Am7 F |C   G

Your love. It's Your love. God, ___ I know…

Outro

    |Am7   F

Your love is never end - ing,

 |C   G

Your love is never fail - ing.

    |Am7   F |C G |Fsus2 ||

It's Your love, Your love, Your love.

Overcomer

Words and Music by Chris Stevens,
Ben Glover and David Garcia

Tune down 1/2 step:
(low to high) E♭-A♭-D♭-G♭-B♭-E♭

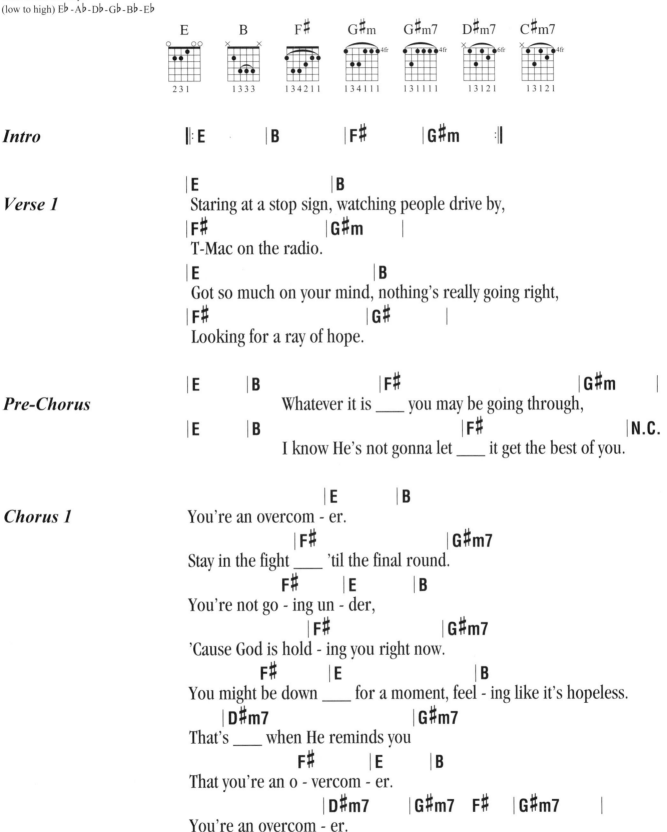

Intro

‖: E |B |F♯ |G♯m   :‖

Verse 1

|E |B
Staring at a stop sign, watching people drive by,
|F♯ |G♯m |
T-Mac on the radio.
|E |B
Got so much on your mind, nothing's really going right,
|F♯ |G♯ |
Looking for a ray of hope.

Pre-Chorus

|E |B |F♯ |G♯m |
Whatever it is ___ you may be going through,
|E |B |F♯ |N.C.
I know He's not gonna let ___ it get the best of you.

Chorus 1

                    |E |B
You're an overcom - er.
            |F♯ |G♯m7
Stay in the fight ___ 'til the final round.
      |F♯ |E |B
You're not go - ing un - der,
            |F♯ |G♯m7
'Cause God is hold - ing you right now.
      |F♯ |E |B
You might be down ___ for a moment, feel - ing like it's hopeless.
      |D♯m7 |G♯m7
That's ___ when He reminds you
            |F♯ |E |B
That you're an o - vercom - er.
            |D♯m7 |G♯m7 F♯ |G♯m7 |
You're an overcom - er.

Verse 2

```
|E                            |B                              |
  Ev'rybody's been down, hit the bottom, hit the ground.
|F#                  |G#m
    Ooh, you're not alone.
  |E                          |B                              |
Just take a breath, don't forget, hang on to His promises.
|F#                  |N.C.
    He wants you to know:
```

Chorus 2

```
                    |E          |B
You're an overcom - er.
                 |F#                    |G#m7
Stay in the fight ___ 'til the final round.
            F#     |E         |B
You're not go - ing un - der,
                 |F#                 |G#m7
'Cause God is hold - ing you right now.
           F#      |E                       |B
You might be down ___ for a moment, feel - ing like it's hopeless.
    |D#m7                   |G#m7
That's ___ when He reminds you
             F#      |E            |B
That you're an o - vercom - er.
                |D#m7        |G#m7    F#
You're an overcom - er.
```

Bridge

```
     |E                            |C#m7                  |
The same Man, the Great I Am, the One who overcame death
|G#m7                       |B
       Is living inside of you.
F#    |E                  |C#m7                          |
So, just hold tight, fix your eyes on the One who holds your life.
|G#m7                         |F#                    |
    There's nothing He can't do. ___ He's telling you:
```

Interlude |E |B |F♯ |G♯m7

                         N.C. |E |B
Chorus 3   You're an overcom - er.
                                        |F♯ |G♯m7
                         Stay in the fight ____ 'til the final round.
                                        F♯ |E |B
                         You're not go - ing un - der,
                                            |F♯ |G♯m7
                         'Cause God is hold - ing you right now.
                                        F♯ |E |B
                         You might be down ____ for a moment, feel - ing like it's hopeless.
                             |D♯m7 |G♯m7
                         That's ____ when He reminds you
                                            F♯ |E |B
                         That you're an o - vercom - er.
                                            |D♯m7 |G♯m7
                         You're an overcom - er.
                                        F♯ |E |B
                         You're an o - vercom - er.
                                            |D♯m7 |G♯m7   F♯ |
                         You're an overcom - er.

                         |E |B |
Outro   So, don't quit, don't give in. You're an overcomer.
                         |D♯m7 |G♯m7   F♯ |
                              Don't quit, don't give in. You're an o - vercomer.
                         |E |B |
                              Don't quit, don't give in. You're an overcomer.
                         |D♯m7 |G♯m7   F♯ |
                              You're an overcomer.
                         |E |B |F♯ |B   ‖

Remind Me Who I Am

Words and Music by
Jason Ingram and Jason Gray

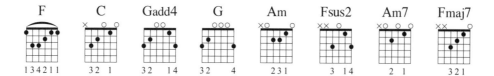

Intro ‖: F C |Gadd4 G Gadd4 :‖

Verse 1

|Am |F |C
　　　When I lose my way ___ and I forget my name,
　　　　　　　　　|G Gadd4 |
Remind me who I am.
|Am |F |C
　　　In the mirror all I see ___ is who I don't wanna be.
　　　　　　　　　　|G Gadd4 |
Remind me who I am.
|F |G Gadd4 |
　　　In the loneliest plac - es,
|F |G Gadd4 Am |
　　　When I can't remember what grace ___ is,

Chorus 1

|Fsus2 C |G Am7
　　　Tell me　　once a - gain
　　　|F   C |Am G |
Who I am to You, ___ who I am to You.
|Fsus2 C |G Am7
　　　Tell me, lest I for - get
　　　|F   C |Am G |Fmaj7 C |G
Who I am to you, ___ that I be - long　to　You,
　　|Fmaj7 C |G |
To You.

Verse 2

```
|Am                              |F
    When my heart is like a stone
                            |C
And I'm running far from home,
                      |G      Gadd4    |
Remind me who I am.
|Am                              |F                              |C
    When I can't receive Your love, ___ afraid I'll never be enough,
                      |G      Gadd4    |
Remind me who I am.
|F                      |G      Gadd4    |
    If I'm Your belov - ed,
|F                              |G      Gadd4   Am   |
    Can You help me believe ___ it?
```

Chorus 2

```
|Fsus2    C   |G       Am7
    Tell me    once a - gain
    |F            C   |Am        G    |
Who I am to You, ___ who I am to You.
|Fsus2    C   |G       Am7
    Tell me, lest I for - get
    |F            C   |Am     G  |Fmaj7   C   |G
Who I am to You, ___ that I be - long   to   You,
    |Fmaj7    C   |G
To You.
```

Bridge

```
              |Am      Fsus2  |C
I'm the one    You      love.
              |Am      Fsus2  |C
I'm the one    You      love.
              |Am      Fsus2  |C
That will be    e   -    nough.
              |Am      Fsus2  |C    G    |
I'm the one    You      love.
```

Chorus 3

```
|Fsus2     C  |G        Am7
      Tell me    once a - gain
      |F         C   |Am         G    |
Who I am to You, ___ who I am to You.
|Fsus2     C  |G        Am7
     Tell me, lest I for - get
      |F         C      |Am          G        |
Who I am to You, ___ that I be - long to You, ___whoa.
```

Outro-Chorus

```
|Fsus2     C  |G        Am7
      Tell me    once a - gain
      |F         C   |Am        G   |
Who I am to You, ___ who I am to You.
|Fsus2     C  |G     Am7
     Tell me, lest I for - get
      |F           C           |Am      G  |Fmaj7    C  |G
Who I am to You, ___ that I be - long    to    You,
     |Fmaj7    C  |G
To You,
     |Fmaj7    C  |G          |Fsus2     C  |G           ‖
To You.
```

30

The River

Words and Music by Josh Silverberg,
Colby Wedgeworth and Jordan Feliz

Tune down 1/2 step:
(low to high) Eb - Ab - Db - Gb - Bb - Eb

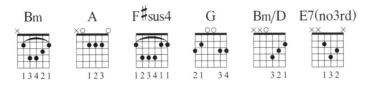

Verse 1

|Bm |A
I know a place where we can go
    |F#sus4 |G
To lay the troubles down eating your soul.
    |Bm |A
I know a place where mercy flows,
    |F#sus4 |G
Take the stains, make you whiter than snow.

Pre-Chorus 1

    |Bm |A
Like a tide, it is ris - ing up deep inside,
|Bm/D |E7(no3rd) |
A current that moves ___ and makes you come alive.
|Bm |A |Bm/D |E7(no3rd)
 Living water   that brings the dead to life, ___ oh,   oh.

Chorus 1

    |Bm |A
We're going down to the river, down ___ to the river,
    |Bm/D |E7(no3rd)
Down ___ to the river to pray.
       |Bm |A
Let's get washed ___ by the water, washed ___ by the water
    |Bm/D |E7(no3rd)
And rise ___ up in amazing grace.
    |Bm |A |
Let's go down, down, down ___ to the river.
|Bm/D |E7(no3rd)
(You will leave ___ changed.)
    |Bm |A |
Let's go down, down, down ___ to the river.
|Bm/D |E7(no3rd) |N.C.
(Never the ___ same.)

Verse 2

              |Bm |A
I've seen it move in my own life,
                    |F♯sus4 |G
Took me from dusty roads to para - dise.
              |Bm |A
All of my dirt, all of my shame
                |F♯sus4 |G
Drowned in the streams that have made me born a - gain.

Pre-Chorus 2

             |Bm |A
Like a tide, it is ris - ing up deep inside,
   |Bm/D |E7(no3rd) |
A current that moves ____ and makes you come alive.
|Bm |A |Bm/D |E7(no3rd)
 Living water   that brings the dead to life, ____ oh,   oh.

Chorus 2

              |Bm |A
We're going down to the river, down ____ to the river,
      |Bm/D |E7(no3rd)
Down ____ to the river to pray.
                |Bm |A
Let's get washed ____ by the water, washed ____ by the water
      |Bm/D |E7(no3rd)
And rise ____ up in amazing grace.
            |Bm |A |
Let's go down, down, down ____ to the river.
|Bm/D |E7(no3rd)
(You will leave ____ changed.)
            |Bm |A |
Let's go down, down, down ____ to the river.
|Bm/D |E7(no3rd)
(Never the ____ same.)

Bridge

         |Bm |A |Bm/D |E7(no3rd)
Let's go down. (Woo,   woo,   woo.)
         |Bm |A |Bm/D |E7(no3rd)
Let's go down. (Woo,   woo,   woo.)
         |N.C.
Let's go down.

Chorus 3

        |Bm |A
We're going down to the river, down ___ to the river,
      |Bm/D |E7(no3rd)
Down ___ to the river to pray.
           |Bm |A
Let's get washed ___ by the water, washed ___ by the water
     |Bm/D |E7(no3rd)
And rise ___ up in amazing grace.
     |Bm |A |
Let's go down, down, down ___ to the river.
|Bm/D |E7(no3rd)
(You will leave ___ changed.)
     |Bm |A |
Let's go down, down, down ___ to the river.
|Bm/D |E7(no3rd)
(Never the ___ same.)

Outro

N.C. |Bm |A |Bm/D |E7(no3rd)
Oh, down. ___ (Woo,   woo,   woo.)
     |Bm |A |
Let's go down, down, down ___ to the river.
|Bm/D |E7(no3rd) |N.C.   ‖
Gonna go, gonna go, gonna go down in amazing grace.

Same Power

Words and Music by
Jeremy Camp and Jason Ingram

Em   C   G   D   D/F#

Intro

|Em |C G |Em |C G

Verse 1

|Em |C   G
I can ____ see the waters raging at my feet.
|Em |C   G
I can ____ feel the breath of those surrounding me.
|Em |C   G
I can ____ hear the sound of nations rising up.
|D |C
We will not be overtaken, will not be overcome.

Verse 2

|Em |C   G
I can ____ walk down this dark and painful road.
|Em |C   G
I can ____ face ev'ry fear of the un - known.
|Em |C   G
I can ____ hear all God's children singing out.
|D |C | |
We will not be overtaken, we will not be overcome.

Chorus 1

|G | |
     The same power that rose Jesus from the grave,
|Em |
     The same power that com - mands the dead to wake
     |C   Em |D |
Lives in __ us,   lives in ____ us.
|G | |
     The same power that moves mountains when He speaks,
|Em |
     The same power that can calm a raging sea
     |C   Em |D
Lives in ____ us,   lives in ____ us.
        |C   Em |D |
He lives in ____ us,   lives in ____ us.

Verse 3

           |Em |C   G
We have ___ hope that His promises are true.

            |Em |C   G
In His ___ strength, there is nothing we can't do.

            |Em |C   G
Yes, we ___ know there are greater things in store.

            |D |C |
We will not be overtaken, we will not be overcome.

Chorus 2

Repeat Chorus 1

Bridge

|C |D
 Greater is He that is living in me.

    |Em |D/F♯   G
He's conquered our enemy.

    |C |D
No power of darkness, no weapon prevails.

    |Em |D/F♯   G |
We stand here in victory,   oh.

|C |D
 Greater is He that is living in me.

    |Em |D/F♯   G
He's conquered our enemy.

    |C |D
No power of darkness, no weapon prevails.

    |Em |D/F♯   G |C | |
We stand here in victory,   oh, ___ in victory.   Yeah!

Chorus 3

Repeat Chorus 1

Outro

    |G | | | ||
           He lives in us.

Start a Fire

Words and Music by Chad Michael Mattson,
Seth David Mosley and Jonathan Burton Lowry

(Capo 1st fret)

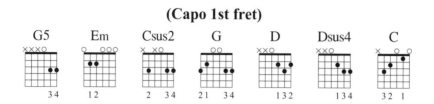

Intro

|G5 | |

(Ooh, ooh,   ooh, ooh,

| | |

Ooh, ooh,   ooh, ooh.)

Verse 1

            |**Em**   **Csus2** |

This world ___ can be cold and bitter.

|**G**   **D** |

Feels like we're in the dead of winter,

|**Em**   **Csus2** |

Waiting on something better.

|**G**   **D** |

But am I really gonna hide forever?

|**Em**   **Csus2** |**G**   **D** |

Over and o - ver again I hear Your voice in my head.

|**Em**   **Csus2** |**G**   **D**

Let Your light shine, ___ let Your light shine ___ for all to see.

Chorus 1

         |G   **|Csus2**
Start a fire in my soul. Fan the flame ____ and make it grow
  |Em   **Dsus4**   **|C**
So there's no doubt ____ or deny - in'.
    |G   **|Csus2**
Let it burn so brightly that ev'ryone ____ around can see
               |Em   **Dsus4**   **|Csus2**
That it's You, ____ that it's You ____ that we need.
                  |G   **|**
Start a fire in me.

Verse 2

              |Em   **Csus2**   **|**
You only need a spark to start a whole blaze,
|G   **D**
    It only takes a little faith.
   |Em   **Csus2**
Let it start right here in this ____ city,
   |G   **D**   **|**
So these old walls will never be the same.
|Em   **Csus2** **|G**   **D**   **|**
 Over and o - ver again, I hear Your voice in my head.
|Em   **Csus2**   **|**
 They need to know, I ____ need to go.
|G   **D**
 Spirit, won't You fall on my heart now?

Chorus 2

         |G   **|Csus2**
Start a fire in my soul. Fan the flame ____ and make it grow
  |Em   **Dsus4**   **|C**
So there's no doubt ____ or deny - in'.
    |G   **|Csus2**
Let it burn so brightly that ev'ryone ____ around can see
               |Em   **Dsus4**   **|Csus2**
That it's You, ____ that it's You ____ that we need.
                  |
Start a fire in me.

Bridge

|Csus2   G |
You are the fire, You ___ are the flame,
|D   Em |
You are the light on the darkest day.
 |Csus2   G
We ___ have the hope, we ___ bear Your name,
 |D   Em   D |Csus2 G |
We carry the news that You ___ have come to   save.
|D   Em   D |Csus2 G |D
    On - ly You can ___ save.

Chorus 3

       |N.C. |
Start a fire in my soul. Fan the flame ___ and make it grow
  | |
So there's no doubt or deny - in'.
    |G |Csus2
Let it burn so brightly that ev'ryone ___ around can see
         |Em   Dsus4 |Csus2
That it's You, ___ that it's You ___ that we need.
          |
Start a fire in me.

Outro

|G |
You are the fire, You are the flame,
|Csus2 |
You are the light on the darkest day.
|Em   Dsus4 |Csus2 |
    Yeah, ___   start a fire in me.
|G5 | |
  (Ooh, ooh, ooh, ooh,
| | ‖
  Ooh, ooh, ooh.)

Thrive

Words and Music by
Mark Hall and Matthew West

Tune down 1/2 step:
(low to high) E♭ - A♭ - D♭ - G♭ - B♭ - E♭

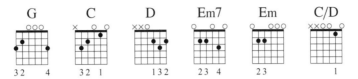

Intro

|**G** | | | |

|**C** |**G** |**C** |**G** |
Oh. _____ Oh. _____

|**C** |**G** |**D** | |
Oh. _____

Verse 1

|**C** |
    Here in this worn and weary land,

| |**G** | |
    Where many a dream has ___ died,

|**C** |
    Like a tree planted by the wa - ter,

           |**G** |
We never will run ___ dry.

Pre-Chorus 1

        |**Em7** |**G**
So, living water, flowing through,

        |**Em7** |**G**
God, we thirst for more of You.

        |**Em7** |**G** |**D** |
Fill our hearts and flood our souls with one de - sire:

Chorus 1

    |C |G
Just to know You and to make You known.

    |C |G
We lift Your name on high.

     |C |G |D |
Shine like the sun, make darkness run and ___ hide.

      |C |G
We know we were made for so much more

  |Em |D
Than ordinary lives.

   |C |G |D |
It's time for us to more than just sur - vive.

|C   C/D |G |
We were made to thrive.

Interlude

|C |G |C |G |
Oh. _____ Oh. _____

|C |G |D | |
Oh. _____

Verse 2

|C |
   Into Your Word we're digging deep,

| |G | |
   To know our Father's ___ heart.

|C |
   Into the world we're reaching out,

| |G |
   To show them who You are.

Pre-Chorus 2

   |Em7 |G
So, living water, flowing through,

   |Em7 |G
God, we thirst for more of You.

   |Em7 |G |D |
Fill our hearts and flood our souls with one de - sire:

Chorus 2

    |**C** |**G**
Just to know You and to make You known.

    |**C** |**G**
We lift Your name on high.

      |**C** |**G** |**D** |
Shine like the sun, make darkness run and ____ hide.

        |**C** |**G**
We know we were made for so much more

     |**Em** |**D**
Than ordinary lives.

    |**C** |**G** |**D** |
It's time for us to more than just sur - vive.

|**C**   **C/D** |**G** | | | |
 We were made to thrive.

Bridge

‖: **G** | |
   Joy unspeakable, faith unsinkable,

|**C** |**D**   :‖ *Play 4 times*
  Love unstoppable, anything is possible.

Chorus 3   *Repeat Chorus 1*

Outro |**C** |**G** |**C** |**G** |
               Oh. _____ Oh. _____

|**C** |**G** |**D** | |
Oh. _____

|**C** |**G** |**C** |**G** |
Oh. _____ Oh. _____

|**C** |**G** |**D** |
Oh. _____

|**C**   **C/D** |**G** | | | ‖
We were made to thrive.

This Is Amazing Grace

Words and Music by Phil Wickham,
Joshua Neil Farro and Jeremy Riddle

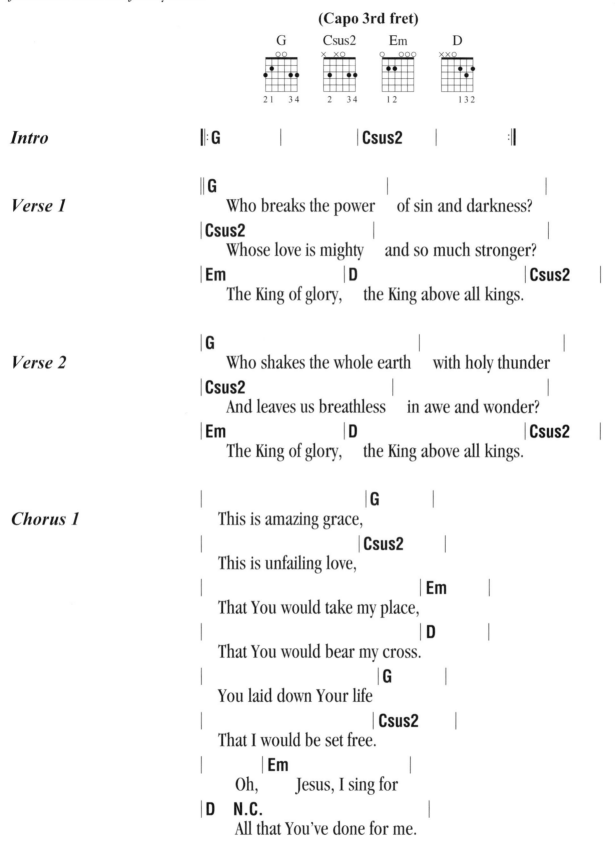

(Capo 3rd fret)

G   Csus2   Em   D

Intro   ‖: G | | Csus2 | :‖

Verse 1

‖ G | |
Who breaks the power   of sin and darkness?
| Csus2 | |
Whose love is mighty   and so much stronger?
| Em | D | Csus2 | |
The King of glory,   the King above all kings.

Verse 2

| G | |
Who shakes the whole earth   with holy thunder
| Csus2 | |
And leaves us breathless   in awe and wonder?
| Em | D | Csus2 |
The King of glory,   the King above all kings.

Chorus 1

| | G |
This is amazing grace,
| | Csus2 |
This is unfailing love,
| | Em |
That You would take my place,
| | D |
That You would bear my cross.
| | G |
You laid down Your life
| | Csus2 |
That I would be set free.
| | Em |
Oh,   Jesus, I sing for
| D   N.C. |
All that You've done for me.

Interlude |G | |Csus2 | |

Verse 3

|G | |
Who brings our chaos   back into order?
|Csus2 | |
Who makes the orphan   a son and daughter?
|Em |D |
The King of glory,   the King of glory.

Verse 4

|G | |
Who rules the nations   with truth and justice,
|Csus2 | |
Shines like the sun in   all of its brilliance?
|Em |D |Csus2
The King of glory,   the King above all kings.

Chorus 2

| |G |
Yeah, ____ this is amazing grace,
| |Csus2 |
This is unfailing love,
| |Em |
That You would take my place,
| |D |
That You would bear my cross.
| |G |
You laid down Your life
| |Csus2 |
That I would be set free.
| |Em |
Oh,   Jesus, I sing for
|D |G | |
All that You've done for me.

Bridge

```
‖: G                                  |              |
    Worthy is the Lamb was slain.
|Csus2                    |                        :‖ Play 3 times
    Worthy is the King who con - quered the grave.
|Em                            |G
    Worthy is the Lamb who was slain.
            |Csus2            |
Worthy, wor - thy, worthy, oh!
```

Chorus 3

```
    |                      |G          |
      This is amazing grace,
    |                      |Csus2        |
      This is unfailing love,
    |                            |Em        |
      That You would take my place,
    |                            |D        |
      That You would bear my cross.
    |                        |G        |
      You laid down Your life
    |                        |Csus2      |
      That I would be set free.
    |        |Em              |
       Oh,      Jesus, I sing for
|D                              |
      All that You've done for me.
```

Outro

```
        |G            |      |Csus2      |
        |                      |G      |      |
        All that You've done for me.
        |Csus2          |            |G        ‖
```

Your Grace Finds Me

Words and Music by
Matt Redman and Jonas Myrin

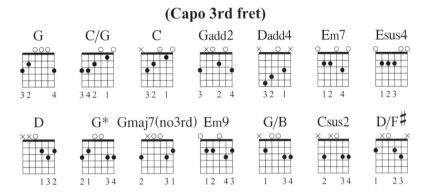

(Capo 3rd fret)

Intro

| G | C/G | G | C/G |

Verse 1

|C |G   Gadd2 |
It's there in the newborn cry,

|C |G   Gadd2 |
There in the light of ev'ry sunrise,

|C   Dadd4 |Em7
There in the shadows of   this ___ life:

Esus4 |D |
Your great   grace.

Verse 2

|C |G   Gadd2 |
It's there on the mountaintop,

|C   Em7 |G   Gadd2 |
There ev'ry - day and the mundane,

|C   Dadd4 |Em7
There in the sorrow and the   dancing,

Esus4 |D |C |
Your great   grace, oh, such grace.

Chorus 1

```
|G*                         |              Gmaj7(no3rd)  |
        From the creation to the cross,
|Em9                        |
        There from the cross into e - ternity,
G/B       |Csus2           |
Your grace finds me.
|                   |G*         |           |
        Yes, Your grace finds me.
```

Verse 3

```
|C                          |G         |
        It's there on the wedding day,
|C                          |G         |
        There in the weeping by the graveside,
|C                  Dadd4   |Em7       |
        There in the very breath we ___ breathe,
        Esus4   |D          |
Your great      grace.
```

Verse 4

```
|C                          |G*        |
        The same for the rich and poor,
|C                              |G*        |
        The same for the saint and for the sinner,
|C                          Dadd4      |Em7       |
        Enough for this whole wide ___ world.
            |D              |C          |
Your great grace, oh, such grace.
```

Chorus 2   *Repeat Chorus 1*

Chorus 3

|G* | Gmaj7(no3rd) |
     There in the darkest night of the soul,

|Em9 |
     There in the sweetest songs of victory,

G/B |Csus2 |
Your grace finds me.

| |G* |
     Yes, Your grace finds me.

Bridge

         |D   Em7 |C
Your great grace, oh, such   grace.

          |D/F♯ |C
Your great grace, oh, such grace.

Outro

     |G |C/G |G |C/G
(Oh, ___ oh. ___ Oh, ___ oh.)

     |G |C/G
So I'm breathing in Your grace and breathing out Your praise.

   |G |C/G |
I'm breathing in Your grace.   Forever I'll be

|G |C/G
 Breathing in Your grace and breathing out Your praise.

   |G |C/G |
I'm breathing in Your grace.   Forever I'll be

|G |C/G
 Breathing in Your grace and breathing out Your praise.

     |G |C
Yeah, I'm breathing in Your grace.   Forever I'll be…

   |G |C |G |
(Oh, ___ oh.)   Oh, Your grace finds me.

|C |G   ‖
     Yes, Your grace finds me.

CHRISTIAN SONGBOOKS
FOR EASY GUITAR

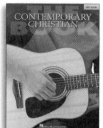

THE CONTEMPORARY CHRISTIAN BOOK

A huge collection of 85 CCM favorites arranged for beginning-level guitarists. Includes: Abba (Father) • Above All • Awesome God • Beautiful • Dive • Friends • His Eyes • How Great Is Our God • Jesus Freak • Lifesong • Mountain of God • This Is Your Time • Wholly Yours • Word of God Speak • and more.
00702195 Easy Guitar (No Tab)........................$16.95

THE CONTEMPORARY CHRISTIAN COLLECTION

INCLUDES TAB Easy arrangements of 50 Christian hits, complete with tab! Includes: Alive Again • All Because of Jesus • Beautiful • Big House • By Your Side • Dive • Enough • Give Me Your Eyes • Hold My Heart • Joy • Live Out Loud • More • Song of Hope • Undo • Wholly Yours • The Word Is Alive • and dozens more!
00702283 Easy Guitar with Notes & Tab.........$16.99

4-CHORD WORSHIP SONGS FOR GUITAR

PLAY 25 WORSHIP SONGS WITH FOUR CHORDS: G-C-D-Em
More than two dozen Christian hits that guitarists can play using just four chords! Includes: All We Need • Ancient Words • Awesome God • Breathe • Everyday • Forever • I Will Rise • Love the Lord • No One like You • Unchanging • more!
00701727 Guitar Chords....................................$9.99

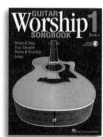

GUITAR WORSHIP METHOD SONGBOOK BOOK 1

Book/CD Pack
This book can be used on its own, as a supplement to *Guitar Worship Method Book 1* (00695681) or with any other guitar method. You get lyrics, chord frames, strumming patterns, and a full-band CD, so you can hear how each song sounds and then play along when you're ready. Songs include: Better Is One Day • Blessed Be Your Name • Breathe • Forever • Here I Am to Worship • I Could Sing of Your Love Forever • Lord, Reign in Me • You Are My King (Amazing Love).
00699641 Lyrics/Chord Frames $14.99

GUITAR WORSHIP METHOD SONGBOOK 2

INCLUDES TAB *Book/CD Pack*
12 more songs with lyrics, chord frames, strumming patterns and a full-band CD that you can use for your worship-playing needs. Songs include: Awesome God • Enough • Give Us Clean Hands • God of Wonders • The Heart of Worship • How Great Is Our God • In Christ Alone • Mighty to Save • Shout to the Lord • Sing to the King • Step by Step • We Fall Down.
00701082 Guitar Arrangements $14.99

PRAISE AND WORSHIP FOR GUITAR

INCLUDES TAB Easy arrangements of 45 beautiful Praise and Worship songs, including: As the Deer • Be Not Afraid • Emmanuel • Glorify Thy Name • Great Is the Lord • He Is Exalted • Holy Ground • Lamb of God • Majesty • Thou Art Worthy • We Bow Down • You Are My Hiding Place • and more.
00702125 Easy Guitar with Notes & Tab..........$9.95

3-CHORD WORSHIP SONGS FOR GUITAR

PLAY 24 WORSHIP SONGS WITH THREE CHORDS: G-C-D
Two dozen tunes playable on guitar using only G, C and D chords. Includes: Agnus Dei • Because We Believe • Enough • Father I Adore You • Here I Am to Worship • Step by Step • There Is a Redeemer • We Fall Down • Worthy, You Are Worthy • and more. No tab.
00701131 Guitar Chords....................................$9.99

TOP WORSHIP HITS

INCLUDES TAB Easier arrangements perfect for guitarists who want to join in the worship service. Includes 30 songs: Beautiful One • Blessed Be Your Name • God of Wonders • Hosanna (Praise Is Rising) • I Give You My Heart • Mighty to Save • Revelation Song • Sing to the King • Your Grace Is Enough • and more.
00702294 Easy Guitar with Notes & Tab.........$14.99

THE WORSHIP BOOK

Easy arrangements (no tab) of 80 great worship tunes, including: Above All • Days of Elijah • Forever • Here I Am to Worship • Mighty to Save • Open the Eyes of My Heart • Shout to the Lord • Sing to the King • We Fall Down • and more.
00702247 Easy Guitar (No Tab)........................$14.99

THE WORSHIP GUITAR ANTHOLOGY – VOLUME 1

This collection contains melody, lyrics & chords for 100 contemporary favorites, such as: Beautiful One • Forever • Here I Am to Worship • Hosanna (Praise Is Rising) • How He Loves • In Christ Alone • Mighty to Save • Our God • Revelation Song • Your Grace Is Enough • and dozens more.
00101864 Melody/Lyrics/Chords.....................$16.99

CHORDBUDDY GUITAR LEARNING SYSTEM – WORSHIP EDITION

ChordBuddy Media
As soon as the ChordBuddy is properly attached to your acoustic or electric guitar, you will be able to make music instantly. Within a few weeks, you'll begin removing some of the tabs and making the chords on your own. In two months, you'll be able to play the guitar with no ChordBuddy at all! Package Includes: ChordBuddy • instruction book • companion DVD with a 2-month lesson plan • and ChordBuddy songbook with 60 songs. This Worship Edition uses songs in both the songbook and instructional book that are geared for Sunday school, praise and worship bands, and more.
00124638 Songbook with ChordBuddy Device & DVD.........................$49.95

CHORDBUDDY WORSHIP SONGBOOK

ChordBuddy Media
This songbook includes 60 timeless Christian tunes in color-coded arrangements that correspond to the device colors: Awesome God • Because of Your Love • Create in Me a Clean Heart • I Could Sing of Your Love Forever • Jesus Loves Me • Kum Ba Yah • More Precious Than Silver • Rock of Ages • Shout to the North • This Little Light of Mine • and more. ChordBuddy device is sold separately.
00127895 Book Only $14.99

HAL•LEONARD® CORPORATION

7777 W. Bluemound Rd. P.O. Box 13819 Milwaukee, WI 53213

www.halleonard.com

Prices, contents and availability subject to change without notice.

1115